SNORT

Giggle

HOWL

Poems to
Make You
Laugh!

To Mary & Jim,
who know how to have a good laugh
—GSB

With thanks to Linda,
who matches each good idea with another

ISBN-13: 978-0-545-01421-2
ISBN-10: 0-545-01421-2

12 11 10 9 8 7 6 5 4 3 2 1   8 9 10 11 12 13/0

Printed in the U.S.A.
First Scholastic printing, April 2008

SNORT

Giggle

HOWL

Poems to Make You Laugh!

Compiled by Gabrielle Balkan

SCHOLASTIC INC.

New York Toronto London Auckland Sydney
Mexico City New Delhi Hong Kong Buenos Aires

Contents

FURRY, SCALY, SPOTTY: ANIMALS & PETS

Welcome to the hilarious world of poetry. Poetry is funny? These poems are. Some might make you laugh so hard your gum falls out of your mouth (make sure you pick it up before your dog does). Some will make you snort or chuckle to yourself. Some might seem odd now, but in two weeks — when you're sitting in class trying to do math problems and your mind wanders to that funny poem you once read, you'll find yourself smiling. . . .

And to start things off with a bang . . . animals! What could be funnier than animals? We're talking poodles here. We're talking ostriches with their heads in the sand. We're talking about the heroic snail, slowly but surely climbing one of the tallest mountains in the world. You'll get a kick out of the motley crew of goofy creatures in these pages.

THE POODLES

Douglas Florian

Poodles have oodles and oodles of curls, while the whirls may have swirls. Which makes poodle boys look like poodle girls. The curls may have whirls, Poodles have oodles and oodles of curls.

CLIMB MOUNT FUJI

Kobayashi Issa

       Climb Mount Fuji,
O snail,
      But slowly, slowly.

      Gaudily feathered,
With nothing at all to say,
I can't stop talking.

A parrot

Jack Prelutsky

ROGER THE DOG

Ted Hughes

Asleep he wheezes at his ease,
He only wakes to scratch his fleas.

He hogs the fire, he bakes his head,
As if it were a loaf of bread.

He's just a sack of snoring dog,
You can lug him like a log.

You can roll him with your foot,
He'll stay snoring where he's put.

I take him out for exercise,
He rolls in cowclap up to his eyes.

He will not race, he will not romp,
He saves his strength for gobble and chomp.

He'll work as hard as you could wish,
Emptying his dinner dish.

Then flops flat, and digs down deep,
Like a miner, into sleep.

AT THE BEACH
John Ciardi

— Johnny, Johnny, let go of that crab!
  You only have ten fingers, you know:
  If you hold it that way, it is certain to grab
  At least one or two of them. Please, let go!

— Thank you, Daddy, for teaching not scolding,
  But there's one thing I think you should know:
  I believe it is the crab that is doing the holding —
  I let go — OUCH! — ten minutes ago!

OSTRICH
Betsy Lewin

The ostrich eyes with eager glint
a stone — his after-dinner mint.
It is a snack that he must swallow
so indigestion does not follow.

SPHINX
Marilyn Singer

If she's lyin'
   like a lion
but she's acting
   like a minx,
She's a sphinx.
If she wearies
   with her queries
and she stares
   but never blinks,
She's a sphinx.
She's a dweller of the desert
   where it's hotter than a griddle.
And I'll bet you she'll upset you
   if you cannot guess her riddle.
So please avoid
   or be destroyed
by such an antiquated jinx.
   (She really stinks!)
She's a sphinx!

SLURPY, MUNCHY, CRUNCHY: FOOD & TREATS

Ever wonder what kings and queens eat? Caviar? Roast duck flambé? Try a healthy serving of nothing but butter and bread! Yes, these poems are about food — some of them scrumptious, some of them nasty. Don't worry; you don't have to eat these poems. Although don't be surprised if you work up a huge appetite belly-laughing your way through the poems on the table.

THE HIPPOPOTAMUSHROOMS
Jack Prelutsky

The HIPPOPOTAMUSHROOMS
Cannot wander very far.
How fortunate they're satisfied
Precisely where they are.
They feel no need to travel,
They're forever at their ease,
Relaxing on the forest floor
Beneath the shady trees.

The HIPPOPOTAMUSHROOMS
Suffer from deficient grace,
And their tubby, blobby bodies
Tend to take up too much space.
But they compensate with manners
For the things they lack in style . . .
They are models of politeness,
And they always wear a smile.

hip-uh-pot-uh-MUSH-rooms

LIES, ALL LIES
William Cole

There is no ham in hamburger,
　　And "allspice" is a cheat;
Applesauce is not a sauce,
　　And sweetbreads aren't sweet.

There is no horse in horseradish —
　　Why are we so misled?
There's no cheese in headcheese,
　　And sweetbreads aren't bread!

O, unlucky man
while eating a shiny apple
you find half a worm.

Paul B. Janeczko

THE NEW VESTMENTS
Edward Lear

There lived an old man in the Kingdom of Tess,
Who invented a purely original dress;
And when it was perfectly made and complete,
He opened the door and walked into the street.

By way of a hat, he'd a loaf of Brown Bread,
In the middle of which he inserted his head;
His Shirt was made up of no end of dead Mice,
The warmth of whose skins was quite fluffy and nice;
His Drawers were of Rabbit-skins, so were his Shoes;
His Stockings were skins, but it is not known whose;
His Waistcoat and Trowsers were made of Pork Chops;
His Buttons were Jujubes, and Chocolate Drops;
His Coat was all Pancakes with Jam for a border,
And a girdle of Biscuits to keep it in order;
And he wore over all, as a screen from bad weather,
A Cloak of green Cabbage-leaves stitched all together.

He had walked a short way, when he heard a great noise,
Of all sorts of Beaticles, Birdlings, and Boys;
And from every long street and dark lane in the town
Beasts, Birdles, and Boys in a tumult rushed down.
Two Cows and a Calf ate his Cabbage-leaf Cloak;

Four Apes seized his Girdle, which vanished like smoke;
Three Kids ate up half his Pancaky Coat;
And the tails were devour'd by an ancient He-Goat;
An army of Dogs in a twinkle tore *up* his
Pork Waistcoat and Trowsers to give to their Puppies;
And while they were growling, and mumbling the
    Chops,
Ten Boys prigged the Jujubes and Chocolate Drops.
He tried to run back to his house, but in vain,
For scores of fat Pigs came again and again;
They rushed out of stables and hovels and doors;
They tore off his stockings, his shoes, and his drawers;
And now from the housetops with screechings descend,
Stripes, spotted, white, black, and gray Cats without
    end;
They jumped on his shoulders and knocked off his hat,
When Crows, Ducks, and Hens made a mincemeat of
    that;
They speedily flew at his sleeves is a trice,
And utterly tore up his Shirt of dead Mice;
They swallowed the last of his Shirt with a squall,
Whereon he ran home with no clothes on at all.

And he said to himself as he bolted the door,
"I will not wear a similar dress any more,
Any more, any more, any more, never more!"

MUMMY SLEPT LATE AND DADDY FIXED BREAKFAST

John Ciardi

Daddy fixed the breakfast.
He made us each a waffle.
It looked like gravel pudding.
It tasted something awful.

"Ha, ha," he said, "I'll try again.
This time I'll get it right."
But what *I* got was in between
Bituminous and anthracite.

"A little too well done? Oh well,
I'll have to start all over."
That time what landed on my plate
Looked like a manhole cover.

I tried to cut it with a fork:
The fork gave off a spark.
I tried a knife and twisted it
Into a question mark.

I tried it with a hack-saw.
I tried it with a torch.

It didn't even make a dent.
It didn't even scorch.

The next time Dad gets breakfast
When Mommy's sleeping late,
I think I'll skip the waffles.
I'd sooner eat the plate!

A diner while dining at Crewe,
Found quite a large mouse in his stew.
    Said the waiter, "Don't shout,
    And wave it about,
Or the rest will be wanting one, too."

Anonymous

THE KING'S BREAKFAST

A. A. Milne

The King asked
The Queen, and
The Queen asked
The Dairymaid:
"Could we have some butter for
The Royal slice of bread?"
The Queen asked the Dairymaid,
The Dairymaid
Said, "Certainly,
I'll go and tell the cow
Now
Before she goes to bed."

The Dairymaid
She curtsied,
And went and told the Alderney:
"Don't forget the butter for
The Royal slice of bread."

The Alderney said sleepily:
"You'd better tell
His Majesty
That many people nowadays

Like marmalade
Instead."

The Dairymaid
Said, "Fancy!"
And went to
Her Majesty.
She curtsied to the Queen, and
She turned a little red:
"Excuse me,
Your Majesty,
For taking of
The liberty,
But marmalade is tasty, if
It's very
Thickly
Spread."

The Queen said,
"Oh!"
And went to his Majesty:
"Talking of the butter for
The Royal slice of bread,
Many people
Think that
Marmalade
Is nicer.

Would you like to try a little
Marmalade
Instead?"

The King said,
"Bother!"
And then he said,
"Oh, dear me!"
The King sobbed, "Oh, deary me!"
And went back to bed.
"Nobody,"
He whimpered,
"Could call me
A fussy man;
I *only* want
A little bit
Of butter for
My bread!"

The Queen said,
"There, there!"
And went to
The Dairymaid.
The Dairymaid
Said, "There, there!"
And went to the shed.
The cow said,

"There, there!
I didn't really
Mean it;
Here's the milk for his porringer
And butter for his bread."

The Queen took the butter
And brought it to
His Majesty;
The King said,
"Butter, eh?"
And bounced out of bed.
"Nobody," he said,
As he kissed her
Tenderly,
"Nobody," he said,
As he slid down
The banisters,
"Nobody,
My darling,
Could call me
A fussy man —
BUT
I do like a little bit of butter to my bread!"

THE MEAL
Karla Kuskin

Timothy Tompkins had turnips and tea.
The turnips were tiny.
He ate at least three.
And then, for dessert, he had onions and ice.
He liked that so much
that he ordered it twice.
He had two cups of ketchup,
a prune, and a pickle.
"Delicious," said Timothy.
"Well worth a nickel."
He folded his napkin
and hastened to add,
"It's one of the loveliest breakfasts I've had."

THE TOP OF MY HOT DOG

(sing to the tune of "On Top of Old Smoky")

Robert Pottle

The top of my hot dog
is no longer bare.
It now has a topping
I didn't want there.

I ordered my hot dog.
I ordered it plain,
without any toppings.
I ordered in vain.

Well, I started eating,
then looked in the air.
A seagull flew towards me
and gave me a scare.

I covered my hot dog
a second too late.
What fell from that seagull's
too gross to relate.

The top of my hot dog
is no longer bare.
It now has a topping
a seagull put there.

BEAUTIFUL SOUP

Lewis Carroll

Beautiful Soup, so rich and green,
Waiting in a hot tureen!
Who for such dainties would not stoop?
Soup of the evening, beautiful Soup!
Soup of the evening, beautiful Soup!
    Beau — ootiful Soo — oop!
    Beau — ootiful Soo — oop!
Soo — oop of the e — e — evening,
    Beautiful, beautiful Soup!

Beautiful Soup! Who cares for fish,
Game, or any other dish?
Who would not give all else for two
Pennyworth only of beautiful Soup?
Pennyworth only of beautiful Soup?
    Beau — ootiful Soo — oop!
    Beau — ootiful Soo — oop!
Soo — oop of the e — e — evening,
    Beautiful, beauty — FUL SOUP!

NOISY, NOSY, NAUGHTY: PARENTS & PEOPLE

Parents and grown-ups — they can't open their mouths without giving us advice! And baby brothers and sisters — will we ever be able to trust them with the television remote control or to leave us alone when we ask? Find a nice spot in a quiet room for these next poems. You'll laugh until it hurts about how silly the people around us can sometimes be.

THE PARENT
Ogden Nash

Children aren't happy with nothing to ignore,
And that's what parents were created for.

NOISOME NAOMI
Jeanne Steig

"Naomi's such a nuisance,"
The neighbors all complain.
"That nasty little numbskull,
She's at it once again.

"Her voice is like a needle,
Her tales are never true.
Her language is so noxious
It turns the devil blue!

"Naomi is a nightmare,
She's nervy as a newt.
Her ma and pa are nitwits —
They think Naomi's cute."

BROTHER AND SISTER
Lewis Carroll

"Sister, sister, go to bed!
Go and rest your weary head."
Thus the prudent brother said.

"Do you want a battered hide,
Or scratches to your face applied?"
Thus his sister calm replied.

"Sister, do not raise my wrath,
I'd make you into mutton broth
As easily as kill a moth!"

The sister raised her beaming eye
And looked on him indignantly
And sternly answered, "Only try!"

Off to the cook he quickly ran,
"Dear Cook, please lend a frying-pan
To me as quickly as you can."

"And wherefore should I lend it you?"
"The reason, Cook, is plain to view.
I wish to make an Irish stew."

"What meat is in that stew to go?"
"My sister'll be the contents!"
   "Oh!"
"You'll lend the pan to me, Cook?"
   "No!"

Moral: Never stew your sister.

OUT OF CONTROL
Bruce Lansky

"The president will come to town . . ."
"The price of beans is coming down . . ."

"I'll love you till the end of time . . ."
"But shooting ducks should be a crime . . ."

"We've never had a better sale . . ."
"We'll have to break them out of jail . . ."

"The Pope arrived to lead the prayers . . ."
"The Dallas Cowboys beat the Bears . . ."

"The temperature is three below . . ."
"These vitamins will help you grow . . ."

What's going on? Well, bless my soul!
Baby's got the remote control.

ADVICE
Florence Parry Heide & Roxanne Heide Pierce

Parents like to give advice.
They'll say it once,
they'll say it twice,
a thousand times,
to be precise:
Should and Shouldn't
Must and Daren't —
how *do* you learn
to be a parent?

There must be very special schools
that teach the parents all the rules,
so they can give their kids advice
about what's naughty and what's nice.

My parents got good grades, I bet —
probably the best ones yet —
A's in NO's and A's in DON'Ts
A *pluses* in Oh-no-you-won'ts.
(They weren't perfect all the way —
they got an F in Yes-you-may.)

I only have one life to live —
my parents want to live it.
If only *I* could give advice,
I'd tell them
     just don't give it!

THE PEOPLE UPSTAIRS
Ogden Nash

The people upstairs all practice ballet.
Their living room is a bowling alley.
Their bedroom is full of conducted tours.
Their radio is louder than yours.
They celebrate weekends all the week.
When they take a shower, your ceilings leak.
They try to get their parties to mix
By supplying their guests with Pogo sticks,
And when their orgy at last abates,
They go to the bathroom on roller skates.
I might love the people upstairs wondrous
If instead of above us, they lived just under us.

DADDY FELL INTO THE POND

Alfred Noyes

Everyone grumbled. The sky was gray.
We had nothing to do and nothing to say.
We were nearing the end of a dismal day,
And there seemed to be nothing beyond,
      THEN
Daddy fell into the pond!

And everyone's face grew merry and bright,
And Timothy danced for sheer delight.
"Give me the camera, quick, oh quick!
He's crawling out of the duckweed."
Click!

Then the gardener suddenly slapped his knee,
And doubled up, shaking silently,
And the ducks all quacked as if they were daft,
And it sounded as if the old drake laughed.

O, there wasn't a thing that didn't respond
      WHEN
Daddy fell into the pond!

OOPS, YIKES, YIPPEE: FRIENDS, CRUSHES, & OTHER DISASTERS

Who are these people? The world is full of odd people who do unusual things and strange people who infuriate us and make us shake our heads in confusion. But like the ones in these poems, they can also make us laugh. . . .

MY GRUESOME GILBERT
Jeanne Steig

Gilbert's such a greedy glutton
When he gnaws a leg of mutton.
All his garments are so greasy
They would make a gibbon queasy,
And his teeth are green and gooey,
Oh, so gorgeously mildewy!

Gilbert smells like old galoshes
(Grandma swears he never washes).
Gilbert's generally vastly,
Grandly, gallopingly ghastly.
No, he isn't worth one filbert,
But I'm gaga over Gilbert.

THE FROG PRINCE

Marilyn Singer

Forget a duck or armadillo —
    let a froggie share your pillow.
I hardly take up any space.
I'll chase mosquitoes from your face.
I'm quite a charming shade of green.
I always keep my toenails clean.
I'll sing you songs and tell you tales
    of big bad wolves and hungry whales.
If I should change, you'd surely miss me
So, princess dear, don't ever
                kiss me!

There was an Old Lady whose folly
Induced her to sit on a holly;
    Whereon by a thorn,
    Her dress being torn,
She quickly became melancholy.

Edward Lear

PORCUPINE
Brian Andreas

A few said they'd be
horses. Most said they'd
be some sort of cat.
My friend said she'd
like to come back as a
porcupine.

I don't like crowds,
she said.

A daring young lady of Guam
Observed, "The Pacific's so calm
    I'll swim out for a lark."
    She met a large shark . . .
Let us now sing the Ninetieth Psalm.

Anonymous

EPITAPH FRO PINOCCHIO
J. Patrick Lewis

Here lies.

THE PACKAGE SAYS:
Michael Spooner

Don't hold fireworks when you
   light them; you'll be
sorry if you do.

Folks will change your name to
   Lefty, stick your
ears back on with glue.

And don't drop them on the
   baby; that's a
very important rule.

She'll just stick them in her
   mouth, you know,
and cover them with drool.

DO, DON'T, CAN'T, WON'T: HOW TO BEHAVE AND OTHER RULES

We all hate following rules: Don't laugh so hard that milk shoots out of your nose at the dinner table; no talking in the school hallway; no combing your hair into a Mohawk to go to Grandma's house! With all the rules and manners in the world, it's a surprise anyone has any fun at all. These goofy poems are different. They make fun of the rules so that you can laugh at them!

DANGER: OVERLOAD

Florence Parry Heide &
Roxanne Heide Pierce

"Pick up your clothes,
wipe your feet,
set the table,
it's time to eat.

"Watch the baby,
close the door,
throw out the trash,
and sweep the floor.

"Mail these letters,
set the clocks,
put away
the building blocks.

"Fold the laundry,
make your bed,
sort your socks,"
my mother said.

I swept the baby
with the broom,
threw out the door,
and watched my room.

I washed the trash,
and brushed my socks,
folded the letters,
and mailed the clocks.

No wonder that I got
        confused —
my mother, though,
        is not amused.

GUIDE FOR GUYS
Douglas Florian

Don't slouch
Don't slurp
Don't belch
Don't burp

Don't snort
Don't snore
Don't be
A bore

Don't daze
Don't doze
Don't pick
Your nose

Don't taunt
Don't tease
Don't lose
Your keys

Don't pinch
Don't poke
Don't smack
Don't smoke

Don't laze
Don't loaf
Don't be
An oaf

Don't sneak
Don't snivel
Don't double dribble

Don't punch
Don't box
Don't wear
Smelly socks

Don't lurch
Don't limp
Don't be
A wimp

Don't whine
Don't cry
Just be
A good guy

TEABAG
Peter Dixon

I'd like to be a teabag,
and stay home all day
and talk to other teabags
in a teabag sort of way.

I'd love to be a teabag,
and lie in a little box
and never have to wash my face
or change my dirty socks.

I'd like to be a Tetley bag,
an Earl Grey one perhaps,
and doze all day and lie around
with Earl Grey kind of chaps.

I wouldn't have to do a thing,
no homework, jobs or chores —
just lie inside a comfy box
of teabags and their snores.

I wouldn't have to do exams,
I needn't tidy rooms,

or sweep the floor, or feed the cat
or wash up all the spoons.

I wouldn't have to do a thing —
A life of bliss, you see . . .
except that once in all my life

    I'd make a cup of tea.

CRYING
Galway Kinnell

Crying only a little bit
is no use. You must cry
until your pillow is soaked!
Then you can get up and laugh.
Then you can jump in the shower
and splash-splash-splash!
Then you can throw open your window
and, "Ha ha! ha ha!"
And if people say, "Hey,
what's going on up there?"
"Ha ha!" sing back, "Happiness
was hiding in the last tear!
I wept it! Ha ha!"

I'M IN MY ROOM AND BORED

(sing to the tune of "The Farmer in the Dell")

Alan Katz

I'm in my room and bored
The boredom rain has poured
Nothing to do
I'm telling you
I'm bored out of my gourd.

With video I've dwelled
Four systems, one handheld
For what it's worth
I saved the earth
When aliens rebelled.

I built six models, and
Made sculptures out of sand
Watched eight tapes
And fought the apes
Then led the marching band.

I got tears in my eyes
Days like this I despise
My parents are
Still sleeping and
It's hours till sunrise!

HOW TO TREAT SHOES

X. J. Kennedy

Try seeing through shoes' points of view.
　　Bend ear to hear your sneakers.
They've tongues to talk. At times they squawk:
　　New shoes contain loud squeakers.

Suppose one day your shoes and you
　　Should suddenly change places —
Then how would YOU like being two
　　With feet inside your faces?

Through chewing-gum stuck to the street,
　　Through snowdrifts when it's snowing,
Would you be happy hauling feet
　　Wherever they were going?

Make friends with shoes. Nights when they lie,
　　Tired from your daylong paces,
Be sure you feed them shoo-fly pie,
　　And licorice shoelaces.

A LESSON IN MANNERS

John Ciardi

Someone told me someone said
You should never be bad till you've been fed.
You may, you know, be sent to bed
Without your supper — and there you are
With nothing to eat. Not even a jar
Of pickle juice, nor candy bar.
No, nothing to eat and nothing to drink,
And all night long to lie there and think
About washing baby's ears with ink,
Or nailing the door shut, or sassing Dad,
Or about whatever you did that was bad,
And wishing you hadn't, and feeling sad.

Now then, if what I'm told is true,
What I want to say to you — and you —
Is: MIND YOUR MANNERS. They just won't do.
If you have to be bad, you must learn to wait
Till after supper. Be good until eight.
If you let your badness come out late
It doesn't hurt to be sent to bed.
Well, not so much. So use your head:
Don't be bad till you've been fed.

NEW YEAR'S RESOLUTIONS
Bruce Lansky

Last year I did some rotten things.
This year I will be better.
Here are some resolutions
I will follow to the letter:

I won't make dumb excuses
when my homework isn't done;
when the truth is that I did no work
'cause I was having fun.

I won't fly paper airplanes
when the teacher isn't looking.
I won't sneak in the kitchen
just to take what they are cooking.

I will not twist the silverware
to see how far it bends.
I will not take the candy bars
from lunch bags of my friends.

I will not skateboard down the hall
or skateboard down the stairs.
I won't run over teachers,
and I won't crash into chairs.

I will not do these rotten things;
my heart is full of sorrow.
But I have got some brand-new tricks
to try in school tomorrow.

WE MUST BE POLITE

Carl Sandburg

(Lessons for Children on How to Behave Under
Peculiar Circumstances)

1
If we meet a gorilla
what shall we do?
Two things we may do
if we so wish to do.

Speak to the gorilla
very, very respectfully,
"How do you do, sir?"

Or, speak to him with less
distinction of manner,
"Hey, why don't you go back
where you came from?"

2
If an elephant knocks on your door
and asks for something to eat,
there are two things to say:

Tell him there are nothing but cold victuals* in the house and he will do better next door.

Or say, We have nothing but six bushels of potatoes — will that be enough for your breakfast, sir?

---

*victuals — what writers and creative types say instead of food.

MY DOG HAS GOT NO MANNERS
Bruce Lansky

My dog has got no manners.
I think he's very rude.
He always whines at dinnertime
while we are eating food.

And when he's feeling thirsty
and wants to take a drink,
he takes it from the toilet
instead of from the sink.

He never wears a pair of pants.
He doesn't wear a shirt.
But worse, he will not shower
to wash away the dirt.

He's not polite to strangers.
He bites them on the rear.
And when I'm on the telephone,
he barks so I can't hear.

When I complained to Mommy,
she said, "I thought you knew:
the reason that his manners stink —
he learns by watching you."

READING, WRITING, 'RITHMETIC: SCHOOL & WORDPLAY

These next poems are funny in a unique way: They allow us to have fun with language, words, and numbers. You can always ask your sweetheart, "Do you care at all for me?" but why say that when you can write a poem that asks, "Do you carrot all for me?" These poems will show you how to turn the English language into Silly Putty, juggle numbers like a rodeo clown, and rhyme your favorite words until the cows come home.

DO YOU CARROT ALL FOR ME?

Anonymous

Do you carrot all for me?
My heart beets for you,
With your turnip nose
And your radish face,
You are a peach.
If we cantaloupe,
Lettuce marry;
Weed make a swell pear.

A teacher whose spelling's unique
Thus wrote down the "Days of the Wique":
    The first he spelt "Sonday,"
    The second day, "Munday" —
And now a new teacher they sique.

Charles Battell Loomis

HOMEWORK, I LOVE YOU
Kenn Nesbitt

Homework, I love you. I think that you're great.
It's wonderful fun when you keep me up late.
I think you're the best when I'm totally stressed,
preparing and cramming all night for a test.

Homework, I love you. What more can I say?
I'd love to do hundreds of problems each day.
You boggle my mind and you make me go blind,
but still I'm ecstatic that you were assigned.

Homework, I love you. I tell you, it's true.
There's nothing more fun or exciting to do.
You're never a chore, for it's you I adore.
I wish that our teacher would hand you out more.

Homework, I love you. You thrill me inside.
I'm filled with emotions, I'm fit to be tied.
I cannot complain when you frazzle my brain.
Of course, that's because I'm completely insane.

SMART
Shel Silverstein

My dad gave me one dollar bill
'Cause I'm his smartest son,
And I swapped it for two shiny quarters
'Cause two is more than one!

And then I took the quarters
And traded them to Lou
For three dimes — I guess he don't know
That three is more than two!

Just then, along came old blind Bates
And just 'cause he can't see
He gave me four nickels for my three dimes,
And four is more than three!

And I took the nickels to Hiram Coombs
Down at the seed-feed store,
And the fool gave me five pennies for them,
And five is more than four!

And then I went and showed my dad,
And he got red in the cheeks
And closed his eyes and shook his head —
Too proud of me to speak!

PARDON MY YARDSTICK

J. Patrick Lewis

A yardstick is how many inches long?
Take half of that.
Subtract the number of lives
Of any given cat.
Now add the number of eggs
In a normal egg carton.
Subtract the average age
Of a kid in kindergarten.
Add the syllable at the end of
TIMBUK _____.

I ended up with half a yardstick.
How about you?

SHOULD ALL OF THIS COME TRUE

X. J. Kennedy

If combs could brush their teeth,
If a needle's eye shed tears,
If bottles craned their necks,
If corn pricked up its ears,

If triangles held their sides
And laughed, if down the street
A mile like a millipede
Ran by on wavy feet,

If cans of laundry lye
Declared they tell no fibs,
If baked potatoes dug
Umbrella in the ribs,

If sheets of rain were starched,
If a brook, with mutterings,
Rolled over in its bed
With a deep creek of springs,

Should all of this come true
And all time were to pass,
Then you could slice a piece of cheese
With any blade of grass.

CLASSROOM
James Stevenson

When   I
r a i s e d   my hand
in   class,   it   didn't
mean   I   knew   the   answer.   Far
from it.   I was hoping the   answer
might   fly by,   and   I   could
catch   it   like   a
b u t -   terfly..

SINGING, SPORTING, SNEEZING: MIXED BAG OF TALENTS & BEHAVIORS

Here's the best for last. The final section is one seriously silly grab bag of performance: acrobats trying not to sneeze as they glide through the air, and cowboys getting their hip-hip on. Ever been to the doctor with a pain in your bones? A poem in these pages proposes that to get rid of the pain, just get rid of your bones! These poems will bring your humorous trek through the world of laugh-out-loud poetry to an uproarious end!

from GOLDILOCKS AND THE THREE BEARS

Roald Dahl

This famous wicked little tale
Should never have been put on sale.
It is a mystery to me
Why loving parents cannot see
That this is actually a book
About a brazen little crook.
Had I the chance I wouldn't fail
To clap young Goldilocks in jail.
Now just you imagine how'd *you'd* feel
If you had cooked a lovely meal,
Delicious porridge, steaming hot
Fresh coffee in the coffee-pot,
With maybe toast and marmalade,
The table beautifully laid,
One place for you and one for dad,
Another place for your little lad.
Then dad cried, "Golly-gosh! Gee-whiz!
"Oh cripes! How hot this porridge is!
"Let's take a walk along the street
"Until it's cool enough to eat."

. . .

No sooner are you down the road
Than Goldilocks, that little toad,
That nosey thieving little louse,
Comes sneaking in your empty house.
She looks around. She quickly notes
Three bowls brimful of porridge oats.
And while still standing on her feet,
She grabs a spoon and starts to eat.
I say again, how *would* you feel
If you had made this lovely meal
And some delinquent little tot
Broke in and gobbled up the lot?

But wait! That's not the worst of it!
Now comes the most distressing bit.
. . .
You have collected lovely things
Like gilded cherubs wearing wings,
. . .
But your most special valued treasure,
The piece that gives you endless pleasure,
Is one small children's dining-chair,
Elizabethan, very rare.
It is in fact your joy and pride,
Passed down to you on Grandma's side.
But Goldilocks, like many freaks,

Does not appreciate antiques.
She doesn't care, she doesn't mind,
And now she plonks her fat behind
Upon this dainty precious chair,
And crunch! It busts beyond repair.
A nice girl would at once exclaim,
"Oh dear! Oh heavens! What a shame!"
Not Goldie. She begins to swear.
She bellows, "What a lousy chair!"
And uses *one* disgusting word
That luckily you've never heard.
(I dare not write it, even hint it.
Nobody would ever print it.)
You'd think by now this little skunk
Would have the sense to do a bunk.
But no. I very much regret
She hasn't nearly finished yet.

THE ACROBATS
Shel Silverstein

I'll swing
By my ankles,
She'll cling
To your knees
As you hang
By your nose
From a high-up
Trapeze.
But just one thing, please,
As we float through the breeze —
Don't sneeze.

GOOD SPORTSMANSHIP
Richard Armour

Good sportsmanship we hail, we sing,
    It's always pleasant when you spot it.
There's only one unhappy thing:
    You have to lose to prove you've got it.

COWBOY RAP
Judy Young

I wanna be a cowboy, I wanna ride a horse,
So I went to the boss man and I told him this of course.
He asked me could I ride, and he asked me other things,
But the last thing that he asked me is he asked me could
    I sing.

      I gave a little smile and a yippee yippee yea,
      And the boss man said I'd do, and he hired me
        right away.
      He told me cows are restless when night is dark
        and deep,
      And said that it was up to me to sing them cows
        to sleep.

We rode across the prairie, we rode the whole day long,
And sitting in the saddle, I thought up my sweet song.
And when the stars came out, with my lasso 'cross my
    lap,
I rode out with them cows and I started up my rap.

With a scritch,
And a scratch,
And loud noises by the batch,
I called out to them cows,
All you mammas hear me now!
Chew your cud,
In the mud,
Don't you worry 'bout no thing.
Swing your cute,
Little tails,
To the rhythm that I sing.

All them cows started mooin', I thought they liked my
lead,
But the next thing I knew, they had started to stampede.
The boss man, he was angry, he said, "Son, you're gonna
change.
Tomorrow when you sing, just sing home, home on the
range!"

BONES
Walter de la Mare

Said Mr. Smith, "I really cannot
    Tell you, Dr. Jones —
The most peculiar pain I'm in —
    I think it's in my bones."

Said Dr. Jones, "Oh, Mr. Smith,
    That's nothing. Without a doubt
We have a simple cure for that;
    It is to take them out."

He laid forthwith poor Mr. Smith
    Close-clamped upon the table,
And, cold as stone, took out his bone
    As fast as he was able.

And Smith said, "Thank you, thank you, thank you,"
    And wished him a good-day;
And with his parcel 'neath his arm
    He slowly moved away.

Even with insects —
some can sing,
some can't.

Kobayashi Issa

There was a Young Lady whose chin,
Resembled the point of a pin;
So she had it made sharp,
and purchased a harp,
And played several tunes with her chin.

Edward Lear

ADVENTURES OF ISABEL

Ogden Nash

Isabel met an enormous bear;
Isabel, Isabel, didn't care.
The bear was hungry, the bear was ravenous,
The bear's big mouth was cruel and cavernous.
The bear said, Isabel, glad to meet you,
How do, Isabel, now I'll eat you!
Isabel, Isabel, didn't worry,
Isabel didn't scream or scurry.
She washed her hand and she straightened her hair up.
Then Isabel quietly ate the bear up.

Once on a night as black as pitch
Isabel met a wicked old witch,
The witch's face was cross and wrinkled,
The witch's gums with teeth were sprinkled.
Ho, ho, Isabel! the old witch crowed,
I'll turn you into an ugly toad!
Isabel, Isabel, didn't worry,
Isabel didn't scream or scurry.
She showed no rage and she showed no rancor,
But she turned the witch into milk and drank her.

Isabel met a hideous giant,
Isabel continued self-reliant.
The giant was hairy, the giant was horrid,
He had one eye in the middle of his forehead.
Good morning, Isabel, the giant said,
I'll grind your bones to make my bread.
Isabel, Isabel, didn't worry,
Isabel didn't scream or scurry.
She nibbled the zwieback she always fed off,
And when it was gone, she cut the giant's head off.

Isabel met a troublesome doctor,
He punched and he poked till he really shocked her.
The doctor's talk was of coughs and chills
And the doctor's satchel bulged with pills.
The doctor said unto Isabel,
Swallow this, it will make you well.
Isabel, Isabel, didn't worry,
Isabel didn't scream or scurry.
She took those pills from the pill-concocter,
And Isabel calmly cured the doctor.

I MET A RAT OF CULTURE

Jack Prelutsky

I met a rat of culture
who was elegantly dressed
in a pair of velvet trousers
and a silver-buttoned vest,
he related ancient proverbs
and recited poetry,
he spoke a dozen languages,
eleven more than me.

That rat was perspicacious,
and had cogent things to say
on bionics, economics,
hydroponics, and ballet,
he instructed me in sculpture,
he shed light on keeping bees,
then he painted an acrylic
of an abstract view of cheese.

He had circled the equator,
he had visited the poles,
he extolled the art of sailing
while he baked assorted rolls,
he wove a woolen carpet

and he shaped a porcelain pot,
then he sang an operetta
while he danced a slow gavotte.

He was versed in jet propulsion,
an authority on trains,
all of botany and baseball
were contained within his brains,
he knew chemistry and physics,
he had taught himself to sew,
to my knowledge, there was nothing
that rodent did not know.

He was vastly more accomplished
than the billions of his kin,
he performed a brief sonata
on a tiny violin,
but he squealed and promptly vanished
at the entrance of my cat,
for despite his erudition,
he was nothing but a rat.

PERMISSIONS AND ACKNOWLEDGMENTS

INDEX